Leasing Digital Tablets / Gadgets To Undergraduates

Jack's Curated Business Idea

By Jack Lookman

Leasing Digital Tablets / Gadgets To Undergraduates

Jack's Curated Business Idea

A. PREAMBLE

In this digital age that we find ourselves; those without digital devices could quite easily become disadvantaged.

Activities, which an owner of a digital device could accomplish in an hour, might take days or weeks to be achieved by those without such device.

Effectively, there's great disadvantage to such individuals, community and probably globally.

The disadvantaged persons may have untapped value just because of this simple disadvantage.

Jack Lookman explores a possible solution to this problem, with the hope of stimulating further thoughts in the reader.

Who knows? This could end up a solution to wider problems.

Have a great read.

Ire awawa ri o. (May you find the blessings that you desire)

Ire kabiti (I wish you loads of blessings)

Olayinka Carew aka Jack Lookman

A Jack Lookman Limited 2023 product

B. ACKNOWLEDGEMENT

The foundational sacrifices of my parents are much appreciated.

I was fortified with spiritual and academic knowledge and practices; as well as great life skills.

Contributions of John Tosin Adekunle are appreciated.

My beautiful Tolu Mayowa Tobi you are very much appreciated.

To all those who've added value to me, I say, thank you.

Most of all, acknowledgement and gratitude to my Creator and Sustainer: Alhamdu lillahi rabbi alAAalameena.

jacksempowerment.com.   jacklookman.co.uk.   jaaloo.com

C. DEDICATION

This piece of work is dedicated to all my family members.

My Late Dad

My Mum

My Siblings

My Children

May Allah grant us goodness in this world and the hereafter and protect us from all torment. Ameen.

jacksempowerment.com.   jacklookman.co.uk.   jaaloo.com

CONTENT

jacksempowerment.com. **jacklookman.co.uk**.
jaaloo.com

1. Introduction

Greetings to one and all. Welcome to our series on Jack's Curated Business Ideas the theme for today is: *'Leasing Digital Tablets / Gadgets To Undergraduates.'*

Let's start with a brief introduction.

- For creative and entrepreneurial minds, ideas could come from anywhere.

- This idea came from a discussion with one of my mentees.

- He mentioned his activity for the day, and I smelt an entrepreneurial opportunity.

- This is just an idea that requires refinement and perfection but at least, it's a starting point.

2. What is the idea?

The idea is about empowering undergraduates in deprived countries

- By providing digital gadgets to make them more competitive

- Make the learning experience more effective.

- As well as explore opportunities that may result from these.

jacksempowerment.com. jacklookman.co.uk. jaaloo.com

3. What's the inspiration for the idea?

- I was having a chat with a mentee.
- He mentioned that he'd be returning the computer that he borrowed
- One that he used it for his final year project.
- He is brainy and has a lot of potential
- But can't afford a digital device.
- This got my entrepreneurial mind working.

4. Who needs the product or service?

- Undergraduates in Nigeria
- Undergraduates in Africa.
- And other disadvantaged countries could benefit from this.

jacksempowerment.com. jacklookman.co.uk. jaaloo.com

5. What are the target demographics?

The target demographics for the end product are:

- Undergraduates in Nigeria
- And other African countries
- Or in other suitable countries.

- It could also be extended to lecturers
- And interested non-academic staff.

6. What business model will be employed?

- Should this idea become a business ?
- Or a philanthropic venture?
- Or should it be a hybrid?
- Should it be administered or funded by:
    o the University?
    o By government?
    o By non governmental organisations?
    o Or a combination of the above?
- This needs to be brainstormed.
- All options need to be thoroughly examined
- And the best solution should be executed.

7. What collateral should be used?

It could be:
- Certificate
- Guarantor/s

This needs to be given further thought

8. What is best practice?

- Could you adequate research?
- Is something similar practiced elsewhere?
- Could you learn from such?
- Could you tweak such practices?
- Could you adapt them to your situation?
- Could you brainstorm with your team?

9. What is your budget?

- You need to do number crunching.
- You need to have figures in currency for executing this project.
- If you're going to find investors, this is one of the questions that they'll ask
- Your figures shall be for capital and running costs.
- You may also include a percentage for unplanned expenses
- And may also decide to execute the project in phases.

10. How will you fund this project?

You may explore different options:

- Crowdfunding?
- Investors?
- Bank loan?
- Multi-nationals?
- Businesses?
- Grants
- Payments from users
- Recycled payments from previous years.
- Donations.
- Give back from successful beneficiaries.
- Donations from alumni associations.
- Etc

11. What threats could there be?

These could be:

- Damage to equipment
- Loss of equipment

- Theft of equipment
- Corruption
- Virus
- Abuse of process
- Inappropriate use of equipment
- Lack of power supply
- Crime - armed robbery, etc
- Communication network problems
- Lack of focus by students
- Internet access affordability
- Migration of undergraduates to other countries
- Non payment of the loan
- Fraud
- University Strikes
- Faulty equipment
- Loss of life of students or their guardians
- Illness of students
- The project may negatively impact those who are in related businesses
- Threat to jobs and status quo?

12. How will you manage the risks?

A few threats have been mentioned; these, and others need to be costed and mitigated.

- Could this be via insurance?
- Could it be by having policies and procedures for any eventuality?
- These could be articulated and updated as necessary?
- Could it be, by preventing unwanted eventualities by adequate planning?
- Could it be by having good systems and structures in place?
- Could it be by employing due diligence?
- Could it be by employing best practice?
- Could it be by learning from mistakes, and avoiding reoccurrence?
- Could processes be transparent?
- Could the use of the content on the gadgets be streamlined?
- Or could it be by an application of one or more of the above?

13. What are the benefits of this project?

I shall mention a few:

- It empowers students
- It makes them more productive
- It enables improved quality of learning
- It creates opportunities for side hustles
- It makes students more competitive
- It levels the global learning playing field
- It gives added value to the quality of graduates
- It adds value to the country's gross domestic product
- It's great incentive for students
- Frees up time for lecturers to attend to other matters.
- Saves time, money and resources of going to business centres.

jacksempowerment.com. jacklookman.co.uk. jaaloo.com

14. What opportunities are presented?

Below are some possibilities:

- Improved academic performance
- Exploration of entrepreneurial pursuits.
- Good competition
- Wealth creation
- Improved quality of graduates

- Job creation
- Greater opportunities for students
- Exploration of wider opportunities
- Added value to the educational system
- Monetisation options
- Greatly empowered students
- Etc

15. How will you sustain this project?

- This could be a long term investment.
- Beneficiaries could be encouraged to give back to the initiative.
- Taxes could be introduced directly or indirectly.
- They could be made to pay back over a period.
- Affordable deductions could be made directly from their employment.
- Systems and structures should be put in place to make it work.
- The idea should be given greater thought and perfected.
- If transparency is exhibited and results are evident the likelihood of investment by well-wishers and suitable others, becomes greater.

16. Here are some costing considerations

- Logistics
- Purchases
- Tax
- Human resources
- Administration
- Insurance
- Write-offs / bad debt
- Discounts to students
- Storage
- Etc

17. What will be your considerations for pricing?

- Costs
- Discounts
- Profits?
- Return on investment?
- Benefits?
- Affordability

- Etc

jacksempowerment.com. jacklookman.co.uk. jaaloo.com

18. What are your thoughts?

- Is it a good idea?
- Is it relevant?
- Is it fit for purpose?
- Is it unworkable?
- Could the idea be perfected?
- Is it a waste of resources?

19. A bit about mailing lists

- One of the offshoots of the administering dispensation is that that there could be a database of users.
- Such information is a valuable asset for marketers.
- They could market and re-market to the mailing list.
- This could be done over several years
- But this needs to be done within limits.
  - o Be mindful of legal expectations
  - o For example, if your potential client migrates to Europe.

- The general data protection regulation needs to be complied-with.

20. What problem are you solving?

- You're empowering those who can't afford digital devices.
- You're encouraging a level playing field on the world stage.
- You're creating a platform for students to do side hustles.
- You're promoting entrepreneurship.
- You're encouraging a more user-friendly learning environment.
- Academic performances could improve.
- Students could become more enlightened.
- Resources could become more effectively spent.
- University ratings could become higher
- Etc

21. Some thoughts on administration

- Documentation and record keeping are important.
- Use suitable software
- Back up information on multiple platforms

- Dispensations need to be done in an orderly manner.
- The process needs to be effectively managed.
- Quality staff are essential.
- Adequate training shall be provided

  jacksempowerment.com. jacklookman.co.uk. jaaloo.com

22. Some logistics thoughts

- Sourcing of the gadgets
- Distribution to end users
- Imports from reputable suppliers
- Software installations by reputable personnel
- Quality control checks etc

23. The value chain

Here are some suggestions:

- Legal professionals
- Logistics professionals
- Engineers
- Technicians
- Insurers
- Administrators

- Purchasers or buyers
- Suppliers
- University staff
- Information technology professionals
- Accountant
- Investors
- Entrepreneurs
- Non governmental organisations
- Collaborators
- Etc.

24. Return on investment

- This shall depend on the business model as well as the aim of doing it.
- The returns could be long or short term.
- The returns could either be obvious or hidden.
- It could benefit the economy directly or indirectly
- It could add value to society.
- It could bring people out of poverty.
- It could positively impact the world.

- The return on investment could be much more than money.
- In addition to economic benefits, it could have social and other benefits.
- Benefits could outlive generations
- Such returns may be immeasurable.

25. Some legalities to ponder

- Terms and Conditions
- Disclaimer/ indemnification as necessary
- Contracts between concerned parties
- Intellectual right issues
- Ownership of gadgets
- Ownership of content on the gadget
- Management of any possible legal issues
- Updating legal documents as necessary
- These shall be done digitally and shall be a precondition for handing over the gadget to the student.

26. Different applications of this idea

- The digital device could be sold to students at discounted prices.

- Entrepreneurs could sell devices.
- Community groups could gift it or subsidise the cost.
- There could be suitable payment plans.
- Discounts could be given based on improved academic performances.
- The gadget could be part of the welcome gift.
- Philanthropists could pay for this.
- Payments by students could be deferred.
- Their certificates could be the collateral
- Etc

jacksempowerment.com. jacklookman.co.uk. jaaloo.com

27. Process Review

- Processes shall be reviewed periodically.
- Reflect on what works, and what doesn't.
- Take necessary action.
- Mitigate any risks.
- Perfect the value proposition.
- Learn and act on experience.

28. Business plan

- Give thought to the processes involved.

- Brainstorm on all aspects of the business.
- Mitigate any threats and risks.
- Put systems and structures in place.
- Purchase gadgets in bulk for economic reasons.
- Ensure that they are of great value.
- Install relevant software and anti viruses.
- Use software to ensure that only the intended users could use it.
- Do adequate administration.
- Put legalities in place.
- Articulate Terms and Conditions.
- Monitor the use of gadgets.
- Track all devices.
- Have relevant insurance.
- After the students have fully paid, remove all tracking
- Incentives should be sandwiched as necessary.
- For students who wish to return the gadget.
  - o Do technical checks and reimburse or charge as necessary.
- Etc

jacksempowerment.com. jacklookman.co.uk. jaaloo.com

29. Why should it benefit only students?

- A similar system could be created for lecturers and interested non academic staff.
- Adjust the Terms and Conditions as necessary.

30. Disclaimer

- This is an intellectual piece.
- Though the idea seems great, nothing is guaranteed in anyway.
- You need to carry out your due diligence before applying the principles.
- We take no responsibility for any outcomes.
- Apply the idea as necessary and modify it to suit your purpose.

31. Could the process be monetised?

- Yes, it could.
- Once the process is fit for purpose, you could monetise the experience.
- You could create content.
- This could be in different formats text, audio, video, etc
- And could be on different platforms.
  - o Social media

- o   blog
- o   podcast
- o   ebooks
- o   paperbacks
- o   etc
- It could also be in languages of choice.
- You could do public speaking and share the experience
  - this could include the good, the bad and the ugly.
  - It could include successes, challenges and pitfalls
  - such content shall be beneficial to the relevant audience.
  - It shall save the time and resources from starting the process afresh
- In the process of sharing your experience.
  - Your learning could increase.
  - Some questions will challenge your doing.
  - Some fresh ideas could emerge
  - And you could end up even better than before

jacksempowerment.com. jacklookman.co.uk. jaaloo.com

32. Why have you chosen only university students?

- In my opinion, academia is the bedrock of any society.

- Intellectuals could find solutions to problems and could add great value to society
- By investing in university undergraduates.
  - You'll not only be investing in them or their families
  - But in community, society, country and indeed the world.
  - It's an investment that could yield multiple rewards.

33. Could the gadget be paid-for, in full at the discounted prices.

- Yes it could.
- However, each student shall be eligible for one gadget.

34. What shall be the technical specifications of each gadget?

- This shall be decided by the relevant authorities.
- It shall be fit for purpose, as well as within budget.
- There could be different specifications at different price plans.

35. Is this idea only for university academics?

- No, it's not.
- I used 'university' for ease of reference.
- It could be executed in other academic institutions as well as other organisations.
- It will however need to be given due consideration and thought, to ensure its success.

36. Who could benefit from this idea?

- Disadvantaged countries
- Undergraduates
- The world
- Families
- The economy
- Entrepreneurs
- Investors
- Collaborators
- Government
- Universities
- Etc

37. Who will fund it?

- Philanthropists?

- Investors?

- Governments?

- Collaborators?

- Multi-nationals?

- Crowdfunding?

- University alumni?

- Etc?

38. Conclusion

- A basic conversation with my mentee stimulated my thoughts.

- I married the possibility of a problem with my entrepreneurial mind.

- If such a perceived problem could be in Nigeria then it could be in Africa and many other countries.

- The concept may or may not be novel but it could benefit individuals, families and nations.

This is Jack Lookman presenting another of the series Jack's Curated Business Ideas. I hope that you got some value and that it stimulated your thoughts. Please feel free to spread the message. Also feel free to check our other platforms:

* jacksempowerment.com
* jacklookman.co.uk
* jaaloo.com

You could also check us on Social media platforms like:

- Youtube

- Facebook

- Etc

Just do a search for Jack Lookman on the internet.

We also have ebooks and paperbacks. You could do a search for Jack Lookman on:

- selar.co

- amazon.co.uk

You could also search for Jack Lookman on the internet.

If interested in promoting our ebooks on selar, please send an email to jacklookman@yahoo.co.uk with appropriate heading and narrative. You'd get about 40% commission of all sales made through you.

Our services include Collaborations, Affiliate Marketing, Mentoring and Content Creation.

The transcript of the audio presentation is available at jacksempowerment.com

Search for *Jack's Curated Business Ideas*

Our mission is to Empower and Inspire Generations by leveraging the Internet.

jacksempowerment.com. jacklookman.co.uk. jaaloo.com

39. On a lighter note...

While I was studying in university so many years ago a colleague, while trying to make a point, or share an idea had difficulty in communicating it.

As he struggled to express himself we came to the conclusion that, **'Idea is need'.**

This was part of the humour that saw us through difficult times. We're sorry for re- Engineering English language.

I hope that I've done justice in communicating my idea.

If not, just remember:

'Idea is need'

This is Olayinka Carew aka Jack Lookman signing off

Ire o (I wish you blessings)

Ire kabiti (I wish you loads of blessings)

About Jack Lookman

Olayinka Carew, aka Jack Lookman is the 1st of 5 Children.
He has 3 children, and an elderly mum. He is resident in the United Kingdom and is of Nigerian origin.

He studied at King's College, Lagos and University of Lagos.
He has varied life and work experiences.
He has been involved in voluntary and paid jobs.
He is dedicating the rest of his life to empowering and inspiring generations.
This is one of his legacy projects.
Though he has health challenges, he does not let that impede his mission and vision.
Even though he studied Engineering in University; his calling is so many miles away from that. He is currently an Entrepreneur, Content Creator, Affiliate Marketer and Mentor.

He is the Director and Owner of Jack Lookman Limited, a registered business in the United Kingdom; and their aim is to empower and inspire generations by leveraging the internet.

OTHER PUBLICATIONS BY JACK LOOKMAN LIMITED

1. *Despair, Submission, Faith and Hope – Volume 1*

2. *Despair, Submission, Faith and Hope – Volume 2*

3. *Monetising Digital Book Reviews*

4. *E-Commerce For Traditional African Attires*

5. *Basic Management And Fundraising Tip For Community Groups*

6. *Monetising A Digital Library*

7. *Ajo, The App And Opportunities*

8. *Empowering Orphans, Widows and Widowers*

9. *Submission, Gratitude, Faith and Hope*

10. *Oro Ishiti- Indelible Yoruba Words*

11. *Eid Monetisation by Leveraging Technology*

12. *What are your thoughts? What is your mindset? - Volume 1*

13. *What are your thoughts? What is your mindset? - Volume 2*

14. *Twenty Curated Business Ideas - Volume 1*

15. *Jaaloo Puzzles - Volume 1*

16. *Jaaloo Puzzles - Volume 2*

17. *Beauty Of The Storm*

18. *Digital Career Guidance App*

19. *Bath Sponge Project*

20. *Monetising Jollof Rice*

FOR MORE RESOURCES FROM JACK LOOKMAN LIMITED, USE THE LINKS BELOW

Olayinka Carew aka Jack Lookman

Jaaloo: https://www.jaaloo.com

Jack's Empowerment: https://www.jacksempowerment.com

Jack Lookman: https://jacklookman.co.uk

Amazon books: https://amzn.to/3jahxEC   (or search for Jack Lookman at amazon.com)

Become a member of Jack Lookman's Facebook Community: https://www.facebook.com/jack.lookman.3

As well as at : Opo Ati Orukan: https://bit.ly/OpoAtiOrukan

Facebook group: Business Ideas etc: https://bit.ly/BusinessIdeasetc

Oro Ishiti- Indelible Yoruba Words - Youtube channel - https://bit.ly/oroishitiytc

Subscribe to Jack Lookman's Youtube Channel: https://bit.ly/JackLookman (or search for Jack Lookman)

Youtube channel (Jaaloo Puzzles): https://youtube.com/@JaalooPuzzles

Business Ideas etc (Youtube channel): https://youtube.com/@businessideasetc5620

Connect on LinkedIn: Olayinka Carew aka Jack Lookman

Or Jack Lookman on Facebook messenger

Email: jacklookman@yahoo.co.uk

At Jack Lookman Limited there are opportunities for mentees, investors, donors and collaborators.

jacksempowerment. com.   jacklookman. co. uk.   jaaloo. com